SAINT ANTHONY OF PADUA

The world's best loved Saint.

By
Rev. Lawrence G. Lovasik, S.V.D.
Divine Word Missionary

CATHOLIC BOOK PUBLISHING CO.
NEW YORK

NIHIL OBSTAT: Daniel V. Flynn, J.C.D., *Censor Librorum*
IMPRIMATUR: ✠ Joseph T. O'Keefe, *Vicar General, Archdiocese of New York*

2 **Fernando's mother taught him to love the Virgin Mary.**

Anthony's Parents

ANTHONY of Padua was born into a world divided between two camps. There was the world of Christ and the world of Mohammed.

Anthony was born on the feast of Our Lady's Assumption, August 15, 1195, and received in Baptism the name of Fernando.

His father, Martin de Boullion, governor of Lisbon, Portugal, was a descendant of the renowned Godfrey, commander of the great First Crusade.

His mother, Theresa, was descended from the kings of Austria. She dedicated her son at Baptism to the Blessed Virgin.

Temptation and the Eucharist

AS a growing boy Fernando suffered many kinds of temptation. It is said that once when he was praying in the cathedral, he was tempted. He rushed up the steps of the sanctuary, made the Sign of the Cross, and cried out: "Fly, enemies of the soul, for the Lion of Judah has conquered, alleluia!" The danger was over; peace returned.

He was firm in fighting temptation. He made great efforts to fulfill the dreams that his mother and teachers had regarding him.

From his earliest years Fernando had a devotion to the Eucharist while serving his uncle's Mass daily in the Cathedral of Lisbon. Jesus in Holy Communion gave him strength to overcome temptation.

Fernando made the sign of the cross to overcome the devil.

Fernando entered the Augustinian house of studies.

Fernando's Early Education

FERNANDO'S parents were members of the local nobility. They sent him to the cathedral school.

In 1210, at the age of fifteen, Fernando entered the Augustinian house of studies, St. Vincent's outside the Walls, near Lisbon.

By entering this community of the Canons Regular he showed that he wanted to become a priest, and thus renounce all claims to his father's title and estates.

He remained with the Canons Regular for ten years; two of these he spent at St. Vincent's and eight at the Monastery of the Holy Cross in Coimbra, the great center of learning. There he studied Sacred Scripture and the writings of the Church.

Fernando Becomes a Franciscan

THE bones of the first Franciscan martyrs were brought from Morocco to the Augustinian monastery in Coimbra. Inspired by such sacrifice, Fernando wanted to become a martyr.

Soon after when some friars came begging, he told them: "Dearest brothers, gladly will I take the habit of your Order if you will promise that as soon as I do so you will send me to the land of the Saracens, there to reap the same reward as your holy martyrs and gain a share in their glory."

In the summer of 1220 at the monastery of the friars of Coimbra dedicated to St. Anthony the Abbot, Fernando received the Franciscan habit and took the name Anthony. Soon afterwards he was given permission to preach to the Moslems.

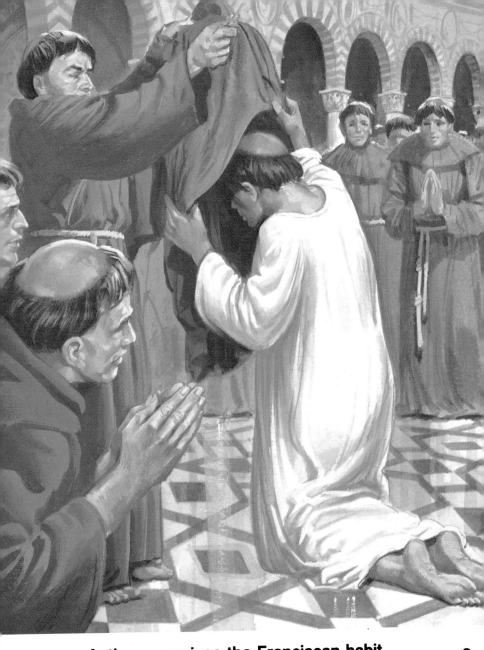

Anthony receives the Franciscan habit.

9

10   **Anthony met St. Francis in Assisi.**

Anthony Meets St. Francis

ANTHONY became very sick in Morocco. In the spring of 1221 he sailed for Portugal. On the way his ship was blown off course to Sicily where he spent two months with the Franciscan friars.

When Anthony was well again he went with the friars to the Pentecost Chapter or Meeting in Assisi, Italy. There he met St. Francis.

When the Chapter ended and the 3,000 frairs were getting ready to return home, Anthony asked to join the friars working in northern Italy. He was assigned to the hermitage of Monte Paolo near Bologna.

Part of the time Anthony prayed and the rest of the time he cared for the needs of the other friars there. Cooking and washing dishes were part of his duties.

Anthony Is Sent to Preach

IN the summer of 1222 Anthony attended the ordination of several friars. The superior asked one of the friars to preach. All the Dominicans and Franciscans present declined except Anthony who amazed the friars with a marvelous sermon on Christ's obedience, even to death on the cross. His talent for preaching was revealed.

Anthony soon received permission to preach throughout northern Italy. He won many converts by his sermons and by his simple way of living.

In 1224 Anthony was sent to southern France to preach the Gospel where the Albigensians had made many converts. He won over the heretics as much by his holiness and great charity as by his learning.

But he failed to bring peace between two warring political factions in nearby Verona.

Thousands came to hear Anthony preach.

13

14 **Anthony preaching from a walnut tree to a huge crowd.**

Anthony the Preacher

ANTHONY surpassed all the men of his day as a speaker. The churches would not hold the crowds that came to hear him. A platform had to be set up in the city square. Soon this space was not large enough for so many people, and the platform was taken into the country. On one occasion, Anthony even preached from a walnut tree.

Shops and law courts were closed on the day he preached. The people came the night before to make sure of a good seat.

Anthony's sermons were so great that he was called upon to settle arguments and make peace between enemies. Judges at Padua asked him to rewrite their laws.

Anthony wrote: "The preacher must by word and example be a sun to those to whom he preaches. You are, says the Lord, the light of the world. . . . Our light must warm the hearts of people, while our teaching enlightens them."

The Spirit of St. Francis

ANTHONY exchanged his beloved solitude for the busy and tiring life of a wandering preacher. He loved the quiet Monte Paolo because of the progress he had made there in the religious life, but he treasured even more the life of an apostle, and joyfully gave himself to preaching.

Because Anthony was filled with the wisdom of God and guided in all things by the spirit of Francis of Assisi, the seeds of his preaching bore much good fruit.

Anthony often had to speak to heretics—men who were misled by the error of false doctrine. He knew that Christian doctrine was all-important, but it was not enough to preach that doctrine to win the minds and hearts of people. Anthony strengthened his words by an upright and holy life.

Anthony in the hermitage of Monte Paolo.   17

Anthony, Teacher of Theology

BESIDES preaching, another task was given to Anthony. St. Francis asked him to teach theology to his fellow friars.

St. Francis said: "To Brother Anthony, I Brother Francis send greetings. It pleases me that you should teach the friars Sacred Theology, provided that by such studies they do not destroy the spirit of holy prayers and devotedness as is contained in the Rule. Farewell."

Anthony began to teach theology to his fellow friars, becoming the first teacher of theology in the Order.

Anthony had been a deep student of St. Augustine as well as of Holy Scripture. He united the teachings of this great doctor with the ideals of St. Francis. This union was to become the special mark of the Franciscan school of theology. Anthony won the hearts of the people.

Anthony was asked to teach theology. 19

Anthony, the Miracle-Worker

ANTHONY served people in their needs of soul and body. Legend has it that Anthony restored a severed limb.

Anthony had a great love for the poor and fed them with bread. He also cured the sick. Legend has it that he restored a child to life.

A visit from the Infant Jesus.

The Infant Jesus Appears

ONE day when Anthony was in his cell, either praying or studying the Scriptures, suddenly the Infant Jesus, surrounded with bright light, came from heaven and appeared to him. Smiling gently He not only allowed Himself to be seen by Anthony, but also embraced him with His little arms.

In memory of this wonderful event, the images of St. Anthony show this holy Franciscan youth holding a lily—the symbol of his innocence—and lovingly embracing the Divine Child Jesus.

Surely it was Jesus who helped him to remain pure and to reach holiness.

Because of his love for the Infant Jesus, St. Anthony attracts children and young people, and helps them to preserve their purity and innocence in this world which is so full of immorality and sin.

Anthony, Devoted Son of Mary

ONE of the outstanding virtues of Anthony was his tender love of the Mother of God. In this he imitated St. Francis of Assisi and his followers.

He was born on the feast of Mary's Assumption, August 15, 1195. In the Church of St. Mary in Lisbon he received the Sacrament of Baptism; and in the Church of St. Mary in Padua his body was laid to rest.

Throughout his life he was always a faithful and loving son of his heavenly Mother. As a famous preacher he also tried to foster the devotion to Mary in the hearts of others. He preached very many sermons on the titles and virtues of Mary, some of which are still found in books. In his sermon on the Assumption, he declared that it was because of Mary's divine motherhood that she was taken to heaven and crowned.

On one occasion Mary helped Anthony in his struggle with a demon.

s a preacher, Anthony tried to spread devotion to Mary.

25

Anthony's Death

IN the spring of 1231 Anthony went with his companions, Brother Luke and Brother Roger, to the friary at Camposampiero. At the hermitage there he prayed and prepared himself for death.

On June 13, 1231, he became very ill and asked to be taken back to Padua. On the way, at the friary in Arcella, Anthony received the last sacraments. Shortly before he died, he called out: "I see my Lord."

Anthony had not been dead a month when the people of Padua asked Gregory IX to enroll him among the saints. A commission of cardinals studied Anthony's life and the miracles offered to show his holiness. Forty-six miracles were approved for Anthony's canonization; only two were worked during his lifetime.

Anthony was brought home to die.

Anthony Proclaimed A Saint

ON May 30, 1232, in the cathedral at Spoleto, Gregory IX proclaimed Anthony a Saint and assigned June 13 as his feast day.

In this same year the people of Padua began building a basilica in his honor. In 1263 this church was completed and the bones of St. Anthony were transferred there.

The people of Padua built a basilica in honor of St. Anthony

Many miracles took place after Anthony's death. Even today he is called the "wonder-worker." He was only thirty-six years old when he died.

Thirty-two years after his death his remains were brought to Padua. The flesh was all consumed except the tongue, which was found red and fresh as it was while he was living.

St. Bonaventure, head of all the Franciscans in the world, was present. When he saw that Anthony's tongue alone had remained incorrupt, he cried out: "O blessed tongue, you have always praised the Lord and led others to praise him! Now we can clearly see how great indeed have been your merits before God!"

The people were happy when Anthony was proclaimed a Sair

The Saint of the World

POPE Leo XIII called St. Anthony "the Saint of the world." In 1946 Pope Pius XII declared him a Doctor of the Church.

Sorrow, disappointment, sickness and even failure had a part in St. Anthony's life. Yet this man was, and is, so attractive that his name has continued through seven centuries in the hearts of Christians everywhere. Thousands of pilgrims from all over the world journey each year to pray at his tomb in Padua, Italy.

And Christians who cannot visit his tomb, find St. Anthony an understanding friend, a friend who will lead them to the Source of his own great strength—Christ the Lord.

More than seven hundred and fifty years after his death, St. Anthony continues to preach the Good News of Christ, feed the hungry, satisfy the thirsty, welcome strangers, clothe the naked and visit the sick and imprisoned.

The Church's Prayer

ALMIGHTY God,
   You have given St. Anthony to
Your people
as an outstanding preacher
and a ready helper in time of need.

With his assistance may we follow the
   Gospel of Christ
and receive the help of Your grace
in every difficulty.

Grant this through our Lord Jesus
   Christ,
Your Son, Who lives and reigns with
   You and the Holy Spirit, one God,
   forever and ever. Amen.